Free Improvisation
A Practical Guide

by Tom Hall

Special thanks to my friend, Lennie Peterson for his beautiful artwork; my wife, April Hall for her endless hours of design and layout, and my mother, Barbara Hall, for the unending support she's given to all my creative endeavors.

Bee Boy Press
Published by Bee Boy Press
Bee Boy Press (USA)
tomhall@freeimprovisation.com
www.freeimprovisation.com

Library of Congress Cataloging in Publication Data
Hall, Thomas
Free Improvisation: A Practical Guide
p. cm.

Includes references and index
ISBN 978-0-615-32862-1

Printed in the United States of America

Written by Tom Hall
Designed by April Hall
Cover Art by Lennie Peterson
www.lenniepeterson.com

CONTENTS

Free Improvisation

A Practical Guide

ABOUT THE AUTHOR

Tom Hall

Tom Hall, a graduate of New England Conservatory, is an improvising saxophonist and music teacher. He has been teaching free improvisation ensembles at Brandeis University since 1997 and has conducted improvisation classes at New England Conservatory, Wellesley College, the Royal Conservatory, and the Rotterdam Conservatory.

Hall has played saxophone professionally since he was 17, performing and recording in a wide variety of musical styles – jazz, blues, rap, rock, folk, funk, meringue and more. What always fascinated him most was not the differences between musical styles, but what they all have in common – the process of improvisation. It was this fascination that led to the development of his theory of improvisation as a universal process that applies equally to all creative endeavors.

He has served as curator for the Cultural Construction Music Series and is the creator and Artistic Director of the Brandeis Improv Festival. In addition to his ongoing teaching and group performances, Hall directs *The Sessions,* a series of workshops and concerts that focus on bringing musicians from all genres together to perform in a free improvisational setting. Hall's most recent project is ImprovLive 365, a daily web-series dedicated to exploring, documenting, and sharing the improvisational spontaneous creativity of life; that produced 365 online episodes, improvisatory public performances, and community based educational programs.

ABOUT THE ARTIST

Lennie Peterson

Lennie Peterson has devoted his life to visual art, music, and arts education. He has traveled the world as a visual artist, performer, conductor, arranger, producer, educator, and recording artist.

His award-winning artwork has been featured in books and magazines and has been exhibited in art galleries throughout the United States and abroad. His internationally syndicated daily comic strip, "The Big Picture", appeared in more than 150 newspapers and was published as a book collection. In addition, Peterson has illustrated nearly a dozen books.

About this book, Peterson says, "I am in constant pursuit of ways to celebrate the marriage of music and visual art. I like to think that what I do visually is similar to what Tom Hall is giving us musically – a free and detached, uninhibited process of improvisation within a basic frame of self-trust. My drawings are rendered spontaneously in a stream of consciousness 'flow' within a predetermined outline of form. In this way, the drawings are very similar to the process of creating improvisational music. For me, it is a perfect visual match to Tom's approach to Music, Love and Life."

INTRODUCTION

Improvisation is elegantly simple. It's compellingly complex. It's plain as day and mysterious as a dream. It's so easy to do that everyone does it all the time, yet so difficult to pin down that no one can say exactly how to do it. There are as many ways to improvise as there are improvisers.

The universe of improvised music is a universe of possibilities, not should's, must-be's, or have-to's. The purpose of this workbook is to encourage exploration of these possibilities by providing a practical way for everyone to explore improvisation.

I believe that no matter what our individual musical experience or goals are, becoming a more competent and aware improviser leads to a more joyful and fulfilling life!

HOW TO USE THIS GUIDE

This book is divided into two basic sections. The first three chapters outline my philosophy of improvisation and my ideas on how to use improvisational exercises in your group's practice. The rest of the chapters contain a variety of improvisational exercises. Once you have played the basic exercises in Chapter Four and feel comfortable using improvisational exercises in your practice, feel free to try any of them according to the needs and interests of your group. I have tried to order each section so the exercises build upon each other, but it is not necessary to do them in any particular order.

As you work with these exercises, remember that each exercise is a tool for focusing your awareness, not a test to be completed correctly. Focus your awareness on a specific thing that you wish to explore and then forget about it. It's a natural cycle of grasping and releasing, like breathing in and out. And most importantly, have fun!

> "It just feels good to be alive when you're
> playing and making up things."
> –Mister Rogers

ONE

What is Improvisation?

From the moment we're born until the moment we die, from the most creative artistic endeavor to the most mundane action, improvisation is an inextricable part of human life. Life is one big improvisation, and every human is a master improviser.

Improvisation seems mysterious because it's a process, not a product; a way of doing something, not a thing we do. Like thinking, or remembering, or feeling, it's both the most incredible magic and the most pedestrian exercise of a basic human faculty.

Improvisation is such an integral part of the way our brains function that it's hard to imagine going through even one day without improvising. Everything we do, everything we learn, and everything we create is a part of our ongoing improvisation with the world. Our very perception of the world is a creative improvisation between our senses, ourselves, and the world around us.

No matter what activity we are engaged in, or what we are creating, the process of improvisation remains the same (as does the joy and satisfaction we get from spontaneous expressive action). For example, let's look at what would normally be considered two very different kinds of activities – improvising a jazz solo, and making breakfast.

A person improvising a jazz solo combines the knowledge and skills they possess:
- knowledge of the composition
- past experiences with that composition
- what they know about jazz
- what they know about improvising
- what they know about music
- their skills at playing an instrument, etc.

With the possibilities and materials available in the moment:
- where they are playing
- who they're playing with
- what the other players are doing
- what has already been played
- how they are feeling, etc.

And spontaneously creates something:
  ▸ a jazz solo!

A person making breakfast combines the knowledge and skills they possess:
  ▸ what they know about food
  ▸ what they know about breakfast
  ▸ what they know about what they like to eat
  ▸ their skills at preparing food, etc.

With the possibilities and materials available in the moment:
  ▸ what's in the refrigerator
  ▸ how hungry they are
  ▸ how much time they have
  ▸ what they feel like eating, etc.

And spontaneously creates something:
  ▸ eggs over easy with cinnamon toast and coffee!

The process of improvisation works exactly the same way in both of these activities. We combine the knowledge and skills we possess with the possibilities and materials available in the moment, and spontaneously create something. This is true no matter what we are doing. Everything we do is a part of our ongoing improvisation with the world and ourselves.

TWO

_____

Setting the Stage

When people get together to do something there is usually an established set of social agreements about what they will be doing and how they are expected to go about doing it. There is a different set of agreements for attending school and attending a sporting event, or for playing in a blues band as opposed to playing in an orchestra.

Freely improvised music doesn't necessarily rely on established musical styles or structures, so many of the common agreements people have about improvising and playing music together simply don't apply. But eventually, every group comes to some kind of mutual agreement about how to improvise together. Whether conscious or unconscious, implicit or explicit, these agreements always exist.

For the purposes of practicing free improvisation, I find it useful to begin with a set of agreements that creates maximum openness and room for exploration. The specific agreements of any group will evolve over time, depending on the interests and focus of that particular group, but the following ideas are a good starting point for exploration.

Every Human is a Master Improviser

Every person has an incredible amount of innate knowledge about the process of improvisation, a lifetime of experience of how to be an improviser! Acknowledging this enables us to focus on the real challenge – how do we access this store of knowledge about improvising and use it to spontaneously create music together?

The Basic Unit in Free Improvisation is a Sound

In most styles of traditional music the basic unit is a musical note. In free improvisation the basic unit is a sound, and a musical note is simply one kind of sound.

Humans are aural creatures and sound is very important to us. We understand the world through the sounds we hear, and communicate through the sounds we make. Each of us has a personal universe of sound, made up of everything we have ever heard and every sound we have ever created.

When we agree that the basic unit of free improvisation is a sound, our exploration easily and naturally includes all of our experience and understanding. Our entire personal universe of sound becomes available to us for use in our improvisation.

Every Sound Goes with Every Other Sound

In most traditional methods of learning improvisation, knowledge of the fundamentals of improvisation and music making are learned indirectly, as a byproduct of exploring a particular style of improvised music. There's a historical consensus about how to improvise together, with well defined stylistic roles and boundaries. This approach creates the idea of an inherently right or wrong combination of sounds, a judgment based on the conventions of a particular style.

Free improvisation is not based on any particular style of music. We can freely choose from all the possibilities of the moment without fear of being wrong or making a mistake, because there is no inherently right or wrong combination of sounds. No musical style is telling us what choices we *should* be making, so we are free to make any choice we want.

When we accept this freedom we also accept a personal responsibility for our improvisational choices. Without conventions to guide us, we must each develop a personal awareness of how the choices we make affect the music we are creating. Does what we play mean what we want it to mean? Did the choice we make express what we want it to express? If not, why not, and how can we express ourselves better?

Tell the Truth

Free improvisation is an expression of self, a statement about yourself and your interaction with others and the world. What gives it life is your own being, and what makes it compelling is that it is a part of your life, an expression of your *being in the world*. You can play the most complex musical phrase, and if it doesn't have this life, it remains just a complex phrase. The single most important thing in this work is truth and authenticity of expression.

Making a commitment to tell the truth, to show ourselves freely, is at once liberating and frightening. There are few places in the world where we have permission to do this without reservation and without judgment. There are even fewer places where we are able to do this in the company of others. Exploring free improvisation together gives us a safe place to totally and freely be ourselves, and to creatively interact with others doing the same.

◆◆◆
Have Fun

It is your life and it is important to you, but there is a reason why they call it *playing* music. Seriousness without playfulness becomes stale and dogmatic. Playfulness without seriousness becomes frivolous and boring.

Allow your improvisation to encompass every kind of fun you can imagine, from goofy silliness to life altering intensity, and everything in between.

THREE

Practicing Free Improvisation

Simply by virtue of being human, everyone has a thorough understanding of improvisation. Everyone also has a personal universe of sound, consisting of everything they've ever heard, every sound they've ever made, and everything they've ever learned. The purpose of practicing improvisation is to learn how to merge these two bodies of knowledge, to figure out how to put together what we know about improvising and about sound, and use them both to spontaneously create music.

One of the simplest, most enjoyable, and effective ways to do this is through the creative use of improvisational exercises. Improvisational exercises are a wonderful tool for exploration.

Each exercise examines fundamental aspects of music and improvisation, providing a focused method of exploring the millions of ways to say "Let's try this and see what happens!"

An improvisational exercise creates a set of boundaries to play within. These boundaries limit our choices, allowing us to focus our awareness on a particular aspect of music and/or improvisation and thoroughly explore it's possibilities. Everything we learn in this exploration becomes a part of our conscious and unconscious awareness; tools in our improvisational toolbox, which are now available to be used at any moment of improvisation.

Staying within the rules of the game requires a certain amount of discipline (which in itself is an interesting learning experience), but don't get too hung up on them. Each exercise is a tool for focusing your awareness, not a test to be completed correctly. The most important thing is to have fun! Play with ideas, try variations. An exercise or choice that doesn't work can provide as much information as one that does.

Improvisational exercises give the conscious mind something to focus on during an improvisation, which allows freer access to intuitive knowledge and inspiration.

Our minds can get in the way of the free flow of improvisation, just by thinking too much. Giving our conscious mind something useful to focus on helps keep it from judging, worrying, wandering, and otherwise stopping us from improvising freely.

Improvisational exercises create a group awareness of improvisational and musical possibilities, a common musical language that everyone knows and can use.

Every exercise we do gives us personal tools for improvising, and gives the group a set of common tools that everyone knows how to use. Shared experience enables us to understand each other's choices better, which makes improvising together easier. Developing a group sense of the improvisational possibilities of the moment makes spontaneous group composition more likely.

Improvisational exercises develop a common language for talking about improvisation.

There is no widely accepted language for talking about freely improvised music. By doing exercises together and talking about them with each other, a group can develop a common language for use in discussion about improvisation, composition, and improvisational performances.

Improvisational exercises can be used by any number of people, in any instrumental combination, regardless of the level of skill or experience.

One of the most wonderful things about free improvisation and improvisational exercises is that we can do them anytime, anywhere, with anybody.

Although improvisational exercises can be used in composition and performance, their main function is to help us improvise better. Be sure to play at least one completely free improvisation in each session, so the group can see how the knowledge and awareness gained from the improvisational exercises it has worked on enhances its improvisations.

Beginning Exercises

The exercises in this chapter are designed to be an introduction to both free improvisation and working with improvisational exercises. They provide a solid foundation for further exploration, no matter what the specific interests or experience of your group.

Tip: Set up the group in a circle, so everyone can see each other clearly. In exercises where players come in sequentially you can simply go around the circle.

In some of the multi-step exercises, it may be useful to take turns having one person give instruction to the group as they are playing, so everyone can move at once and the flow of the exercise isn't interrupted.

Exercise 1: One Sound

Spontaneously creating an expressive sound is the first step to freely improvising, and doing it in a group is a great way to experience improvising with others. This is an excellent first exercise for those that have not improvised before, and a good warm-up for more experienced improvisers.

Step 1: Everyone in the group plays one sound, in sequence, focusing on playing a sound that expresses the feeling of the moment.

Sit or stand in a relaxed manner, and in a "ready to play" position. Focus your attention inward. Be aware of how you're feeling in this moment. Don't make any judgments, just watch and see how you feel. Wait for a sound or an impulse to movement to come into your awareness. Allow it to come through your body and create a sound. You don't have to "do" anything. The sound will create itself if you make space to let it happen. Take all the time needed to feel, hear, and express each sound.

If this seems difficult, bring your attention back to how you're feeling. It's not important what you are feeling, only that you are aware of it. Now play that feeling! Any sound that is a truly spontaneous expression (no matter what it is) is a valued and appropriate response to this exercise.

Step 2: Play all the sounds at the same time. That's the group sound of that moment!

Exercise 2: One Sound at a Time

This exercise series can be done with or without a pulse (a series of beats of equal duration). When doing it with a pulse, count off a tempo (the speed of the pulse). Every person has one beat to play their sound. If someone misses their beat, skip them and go on to the next person. If the pulse breaks down, just stop, and start again. If playing without a pulse, simply play the sounds in sequence.

Step 1: Everyone in the group plays one sound, in sequence, focusing on playing a sound that expresses the feeling of the moment. Once everyone has played one sound keep going around the circle, each person playing a sound of their choice. You can change your sound each time around or keep it the same. Once the group is comfortable doing this, follow the suggestions in Steps 2-5. Give ample time for everyone to experience each step before going on to the next.

Step 2: Direct your attention equally to your sounds and to the sounds the others are making.

Step 3: Don't think at all about the sound you are going to make. Give all your attention to everyone else's sounds. When it's your turn, just do something. (Anything!) Don't think about it. (Just do it!)

Step 4: As you listen to everyone's sounds notice how they come together to make a phrase. The more you focus your attention on this phrase, the more interesting and coherent it will become. You are now improvising a "group phrase" together!

Step 5: Relax your concern about stopping right away when the next person's sound starts. Consider that all the sounds being made belong to all of you, so there are no boundaries between the various sounds.

Exercise 3: One Sound, Anywhere in the Beat

Step 1: Play in sequence around the circle. Each person has one beat in which to play their sound, and can use any combination of rhythms as long as they are within that beat. Go around the circle as many times as you like. If you lose track of the beat, stop, and start again.

Exercise 4: Any Sound, Anywhere in the Beat

Step 1: Play in sequence around the circle. Each person has one beat in which to play anything they want, using any combination of rhythms and/or sounds. Go around the circle as many times as you like. If you lose track of the beat, stop, and start again.

Exercise 5: One Sound, Change Tempo

Step 1: Play in sequence around the circle. Each person has one beat in which to play, and can use any combination of rhythms and sounds as long as they are within that beat.

Step 2: Speed up or slow down the tempo. See how fast or slow you can go without breaking down. See how smoothly you can speed up and slow down together.

Exercise 6: One Sound, Different Feels

Step 1: Play in sequence around the circle. Each person has one beat in which to play, and can use any combination of rhythms and sounds as long as they are within that beat.

Step 2: Vary the tempo, time signature, and groove. What does it feel like to do this exercise in 6/8? In 3/4? In a swing feel, or a funk feel, or straight eighths, or...?

Exercise 7: One Sound, Together
This exercise is done without a pulse.

Step 1: Play one sound, in sequence. Remember what your sound is!

Step 2: Play a group improvisation. Everyone can only use the sound they have just played, but they can play it however and whenever they want.

Tip: Choosing to play silence is as valid a musical choice as choosing to play sound. Anyone can choose to play silence at any point in the group phrase. Trust that if someone doesn't play a sound, they are playing a silence.

Exercise 8: More Than One Sound, Together

This exercise is done without a pulse.

Step 1: Play a group improvisation. Whatever sound you choose to make first is the one and only sound you can use in that improvisation.

Step 2: Play a group improvisation. Increase the number of sounds each person can play to two sounds, or three sounds, or...

At this point, the group is playing textural group improvisation. If you wish to continue with more textural group improvisational exercises, go to Chapter 7: Textures.

Basic Group Groove Exercises

When freely improvising, any player can choose to be a part of the rhythm section. The commonly accepted roles and boundaries that define a rhythm section in more traditional styles of music do not necessarily apply. Any player can be responsible for improvising a background, creating a groove, or otherwise providing accompaniment. Although this accompaniment does not have to conform to any traditional standard, being an accompanist requires a kind of skill and understanding that many lead instrumentalists have never learned. Players of traditional rhythm section instruments have experience being accompanists, but may want to experiment with different ways to improvise accompaniment out-side of their traditional roles.

The exercises in this workbook provide an opportunity to practice many different kinds of accompaniment, beginning with this initial exploration of improvising group grooves. Use these beginning groove exercises to slow down the decision making process, allowing each player to take as much time as needed to find the choices they want to make. Use them to explore basic questions about groove creation: How do different kinds of lines interact with each other? What adds or detracts from a groove? How can a group of people spontaneously create a groove? What are the different parts and roles in a groove and how can I function in them?

Exercise 9: Ostinato Groove

Step 1: One person plays a repeating pattern, in time (an ostinato). This pattern can be *anything*, but it has to stay the same. Take as much time as needed to find the desired phrase and to let it settle into a groove.

Step 2: The second player adds a second ostinato part to the groove, taking as much time as needed to find what they want to play in response to the first players offering. Once the second part is chosen, allow time to feel how the two phrases fit together into a groove before moving on.

Step 3: One at a time, the other players enter in the same way, until all the players are playing their repeated patterns at the same time. You have now improvised a groove! Keep playing this groove until every part seems locked into the pulse in a satisfying way, then stop.

Exercise 10: Mutating Groove

Step 1: One person plays an ostinato pattern, in time. This pattern can be anything, but it has to stay the same. Take as much time as needed to find the desired phrase and to let it settle into a groove.

Step 2: The second player adds a second part to the groove, taking as much time as needed to find what they want to play in response to the first players offering, and to fit the two phrases together.

Step 3: One at a time, the other players enter in the same way, until all the players are playing their repeated patterns at the same time. Keep playing this groove, allowing every part to fit together in a satisfying way.

Step 4: The first person drops out, listens to the groove, then comes in with a new part. Do this in sequence until everyone has changed, and the original groove is transformed into a new groove. Keep playing this new groove until all the parts are locked in. You can stop here or keep going, changing the groove as many times as you like.

Tip: Stay active as you repeat your part. Each repetition is an opportunity to deepen your groove, and to connect more fully with the parts others are playing.

As different parts come in, allow yourself to make small adjustments to what you are playing, as long as it contributes to the greater groove.

Tip: If the groove seems too busy, try having everyone play half as many notes and twice as much silence, or stretch what they have played over twice as many beats.

Everyone doesn't have to make different sounds at different times. You can choose to play with someone else.

It's tempting for rhythm section players to play beats or grooves they already know. Have them alternate this with playing single phrases or patterns instead of known beats. Drummers can experiment with confining themselves to one or two pieces of their drum kit.

Vary the tempo and feel of the groove. If the group seems stuck in one feel, you might need a "palate cleanser" (see page 87). To lessen self consciousness and stiffness, try doing Warm-Up Exercise 113: Human Machine, before doing Exercise 9.

Exercise 11: Dueling Grooves

Step 1: Split into two groups.

Step 2: Group 1 improvises a groove by coming in one by one with an ostinato pattern. Once the groove is established, play it long enough for each person to mark their part in their memory, then stop.

Step 3: Group 2 improvises a different groove in the same way. Once it's established, play it long enough for each person to mark their part in their memory, then stop.

Step 4: Group 1 plays their groove. On cue, Group 2 comes in with their groove and Group 1 stops playing.

Step 5: On cue, Group 1 comes back in and Group 2 stops.

Step 6: Continue going back and forth between these two grooves.

Step 7: At the end, play the two grooves together.

Exercise 12: Mirroring

Some improvisational theater exercises are particularly useful for musicians, either as a warm-up, or to illustrate an improvisational idea. This theater game translates well to musical improvisation. I recommend doing it without instruments first, by moving and making sounds with your body and voice. Then try it with instruments, keeping the same sense of playfulness and fun. The instructions are the same whether doing it with or without instruments.

This duet exercise is great for developing empathy, learning how to lead and follow, and how to begin and end phrases. In its final stages, no one is leading and no one is following. The music itself is creating the music!

Step 1: One person does something (anything!). A second person mirrors them.

Step 2: At the natural ending of each phrase or movement, switch roles. The person who was initiating becomes the mirrorer, and the person who was mirroring is now initiating the action.

If you are having trouble ending phrases or identifying the endings of phrases, try making simpler gestures and phrases, with the goal of making them easy for your partner to anticipate.
You can also have a third person watch for potential endings and call out "switch" when they see or hear the ending of a phrase or movement.

Tip: Do not follow the other. The goal is to mirror them, to be them. Move at the same time they do, like a reflection in a mirror.

Do not try to move in such a way as to "trick" the other player. Part of the goal when you are initiating action is to make it easy for them to mirror you.

The exercise can stop here, or if you find you are able to get into a flow of easily switching roles, go to Step 3.

Step 3: In this phase of the exercise, each person follows the other. No one is leading, they are both following. At this point, the movement itself is creating the movement. The music is creating the music!

Exercise 13: Ending

We all understand endings. Our lives are full of them. But to be able to use them when improvising together we must develop a shared awareness of potential endings as they occur, and a willingness to embrace them.

Something has to end in order for something else to begin. This is true for every part of music, whether it's a sound, a phrase, a part of an improvisation, an improvisation, or an entire performance. Learning how to recognize and create endings together is as important as any other part of improvising.

This simple exercise is great for developing an awareness of endings. It can be done with any number of people, but doing it as a duet gets the point across the fastest. It helps to have an experienced "ender" listen for and point out potential endings.

Step 1: Start playing. Stop at the first potential ending that occurs.

Step 2: Start playing. Be aware of the first ending as it occurs. Choose whether you want to stop or to go on. If you go on, choose whether to play something like the first section or something different. Stop at the second potential ending that occurs.

Step 3: Start playing. Be aware of the first ending and choose whether you want to stop or go on. If you go on, choose whether to play something like the first section or something different. Watch for the second potential ending, and choose again whether to stop or go on. If you go on to a third section, is it a continuation of the first section, a continuation of the second section, or a new section?

Step 4: After you have done Steps 1-3 enough to have confidence in your awareness of potential endings, leave the final ending of the improvisation open.

Once you start to look, there are endings all over the place. All you need to do is let the improvisation have its ending, without any interference from whatever you are personally involved in at that moment, and be willing and ready to end at any time.

Exercise 14: Awareness 1

The exercise works well with long held out notes or sounds, changing slowly.

Step 1: Two players hold out a note or sound.

Step 2: Focus your attention on each sound separately, then hold both sounds in your awareness simultaneously, and with equal importance. Hear both of the sounds, and the relationship between them.

Step 3: Observe this relationship, and your reaction to it. Don't do anything, just watch as the sounds slightly change and subtle reactions occur. Observe your feelings and thoughts. Are you happy with the sounds, or do you want to change them?

Step 4: If you feel the need to change, wait until the wanting to change becomes overwhelming, then allow this desire to create the change.

Step 5: Repeat Steps 3 and 4 until you want to end.

Step 6: Repeat Steps 1-5 with more players. Take enough time in Step 2 to direct your awareness to each players individual sound, and to all the sounds together.

FIVE

Duets
The Art of Relationship

As soon as more than one person is involved, improvisation is as much about the relationship between what's played as it is about what each person is playing. From the very first notes a relationship is established, and the story of the improvisation is the story of that relationship. Duets are an excellent way to begin to explore the complexities of relationship, since the simplicity of two voices makes it easier to hear and understand many concepts.

Tip: Only two people will be playing at any given time, but everyone's participation is important. The players need the attention and input of the listener to get the most out of their exploration, and the awareness and ideas that the listeners gain from actively listening will aid them in their own exploration when it is their turn to play.

Remember that every improvisation begins before you make the first sound. If you are not focused and connected with the other player before you start playing, the beginning of the improvisation will always be about getting connected and focused.

If the duets in these exercises are relatively concise it makes the exercises more effective. If you have not done Exercise 13: Ending yet, I recommend doing it as a duet before going on to the other duet exercises.

Developing Relationship Awareness

Two people playing together create a third thing – the relationship between the two things played. The focus of this first series of exercises is gaining an awareness of these relationships and developing the ability to improvise with them.

Exercise 15: Hearing Relationship

Step 1: Two people play a short duet improvisation.

Step 2: Discuss the relationship between the two players. How would you describe it? Did it change over the course of the duet? If the players were not aware of their relationship have them play another duet, this time focusing awareness on what the other person is playing. Pay particular attention to the choices made at each "ending point" (see Exercise 13: Ending).

Tip: There are many ways to describe relationship. You can describe relationship by using musical parameters. This description can be as simple or detailed as you wish ("He played short notes, while she played long notes." "She played a diatonic melody made up of large intervals. He accompanied the melody with a descending bass line.")

You can also describe relationship using any analogies and metaphors you can think of (" He was chasing me, I was running away." "We were having a conversation, he was getting more and more angry and I was trying to stay calm." "She was heavy, I was light.")

No matter how you choose to describe it, don't worry about "correctly" naming the relationship. Relationship identification is a tool for gaining awareness and exploring different possibilities, not the actual point of the exercise.

Exercise 16: How Many Relationships Can You Find?

Step 1: Keep improvising short duets, one after the other, either with the same two players or with different players. If the duets keep sounding the same, try saying you are going to play "completely different" relationships, or "the opposite" relationship.

Choosing and Committing

The initial offerings in every improvisation contain the potential for many different relationships. An improvisation starts to take shape and make sense once the players have made a choice about which of those potential relationships they are going to explore. This idea of making and committing to a choice has already been in play in some of the exercises above, but consciously focusing on it will clarify the players' understanding.

Tip: Understanding how to make a strong choice and commit to it is an essential skill for every improviser. However, one of the beautiful paradoxes of improvisation is that every individual choice is simultaneously of the greatest importance and not important at all. At every moment you must be both completely committed to what you are playing, and completely willing to let go of it if the music demands it.

Exercise 17: Staying in a Relationship

Step 1: Two players start playing at the same time. Whatever occurs in the first few seconds of the duet will be the only materials and relationship they can use in the improvisation.

Exercise 18: The Same, But Different

Step 1: Two players start playing at the same time. Whatever occurs in the first few seconds of the duet will be the only materials and relationship they can use in the improvisation.

Tip: If you want to improvise in any other manner besides stream of consciousness, it is essential to be aware of the choices being made. Without a group awareness of these choices it's difficult to develop them, improvise with them, or refer back to them. In order to improvise with something, you have to establish it in your own awareness, in the awareness of the group, and in the awareness of the audience. This requires both choosing and committing to those choices.

Step 2: The same two players improvise another duet with the same kind of material and/or relationship as the first. Try using the same materials but creating a different relationship with them. Try improvising the same relationship with different materials. Try using both the materials and relationship from the first duet. Notice how these duets are the same or different from the initial improvisation.

Exercise 19: Other Potential Relationships

Step 1: Two players start playing at the same time. Whatever occurs in the first few seconds of the duet will be the only materials and relationship they can use in the improvisation.

Tip: Switch emphasis between different ways of describing relationships. You can use musical parameters, descriptive phrases, human relationships, relationships in nature, etc. Any relationship description can be the subject of an improvisation.

Step 2: Identify other possible relationships that were available in the players' initial offers but were not developed.

Step 3: Start the duet the same way as before, but explore one of the other potential relationships.

Exercise 20: Choose Before Playing 1

Step 1: Improvise a duet. Decide together what the relationship will be before beginning the improvisation.

Exercise 21: Choose Before Playing 2

Step 1: Improvise a duet. Each player decides beforehand what the relationship will be without telling the other.

Exercise 22: Choose Before Playing 3

Step 1: Improvise a duet. Decide together what the relationship will be before beginning the improvisation, but don't tell the listeners. Afterwards, see if they can guess the players intended relationship.

Exercise 23: One Voice Changing

Step 1: Improvise a duet where both players start playing at the same time. Whatever occurs in the first few seconds of the duet will be the only materials and relationship they can use in the improvisation.

Step 2: Play a second duet, with Player 1 repeating their initial choices from the previous duet and Player 2 making a different choice in response. Do this as many times as you want, allowing Player 2 to explore some of the many possible responses to Player 1's original offers.

Step 3: Play another duet. This time Player 2 repeats their initial choices from the duet in Step 1, while Player 1 makes different choices. Do this as many times as you want, allowing Player 1 to explore some of the many possible responses to Player 2's original offers.

Tip: *This is a good initial exercise for learning how to remember what you have improvised. Unless you bring it to your conscious awareness to "mark it" for longer term memory storage, what you improvise from moment to moment is very often lost after a short time. With practice this skill will become second nature, enabling you to remember and refer back to previous parts of an improvisation.*

More Relationship Fun

There are lots of ways to use relationship as an inspiration for duet improvisations, and I invite you to have fun exploring as many as you can think up. The only limit is your imagination! Here are a few more ideas to get you started.

Exercise 24: Coming Together 1

Imagine relationship as a scale that goes from being completely together, (as in Exercise 12: Mirroring) to completely separate from each other. Any moment of relationship can be found somewhere on this scale. Here's an exercise series for exploring this. Do all three of them in a row. (You can also do this as a group exercise.)

Step 1: Two players stand facing away from each other.

Step 2: Begin improvising. Consciously try to be completely separate by not relating at all to the other person.

Step 3: Gradually move to face each other, while simultaneously connecting more and more with the other person and what they are playing.

Exercise 25: Coming Together 2

Step 1: Do Exercise 23 again, but without making any sound.

Exercise 26: Coming Together 3

Step 1: Two players stand facing away from each other.

Step 2: Begin improvising. Consciously try to make what you play completely separate from what the other person is playing, by being intensely aware of what they are playing.

Step 3: Gradually move to face each other, while simultaneously connecting more and more with the music of the other person.

Exercise 27: Musical Relationships

Step 1: Use musical terminology to describe the relationship you are going to play, then improvise a duet based on that description. Any musical relationship that two voices can have can be explored in an improvised duet. (See Chapter 11: Musical Parameters for more.)

Exercise 28: Human Relationships

Step 1: Any human relationship can be the subject of a duet improvisation. Even a simple description of any common relationship offers a wealth of improvisational possibilities. You can use general descriptions of activities two people might engage in, such as having a conversation or having a fight. You can also give more detail about the characters (two strangers talking while waiting for a bus, a couple having a fight, a parent scolding a child), or provide a narrative arc to your improvisation by making up small stories to play.

Exercise 29: A World of Relationship

Step 1: Play duets based on other relationships in the world (like a frying pan and a piece of bacon, a dog and a squirrel, or a tree and the wind).

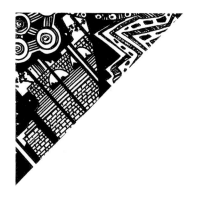

SIX

_____

Advanced Groove Exercises

Here are some more exercises for working on grooves and using grooves in your improvisation. They build on Exercise 9: Ostinato Groove and Exercise 10: Mutating Groove. When you become good at it, you'll be able to spontaneously improvise a burning groove, change it at will, use it as an accompaniment for solos and explorations, and much, much more!

Exercise 30: Starting a Groove Together

Once you are comfortable creating a group groove by coming in one at a time, try starting together. The goal of this exercise is to learn how to settle into a groove as quickly as possible, so don't hesitate to change or shift what you are playing so it works better with what the others are playing.

Step 1: Count off a tempo. Improvise a group groove with everyone starting at the same time.

Step 2: Allow time for the groove to settle into place. Once it feels like it is well established, stop.

Step 3: Repeat Steps 1 and 2 until you are comfortable starting a groove together.

> *Tip: Simplify! Leave space for the groove to breathe.*
>
> *Experiment with playing both inside and outside of the traditional roles of your instrument.*
>
> *Experiment with playing different length phrases.*

Step 4: Once you are comfortable starting a groove together, try this exercise again, but without counting off the tempo. See how fast can you find a groove!

Exercise 31: The Primary Rhythm

Every groove has at least one composite primary rhythm that defines the feel of the groove and makes it rhythmically different from another groove in the same tempo. These are often the most accented parts of the phrase or the beats where different phrases come together.

Step 1: Improvise a group groove.

Step 2: Find the primary rhythm of the groove and play it or clap it all together.

Step 3: Play the original parts of the groove again. Observe how your part interacts with the primary rhythm.

Exercise 32:
The Primary Rhythm +1

Every rhythm also defines the space around it.

Step 1: Improvise a group groove.

Step 2: Find the primary rhythm of the groove and play it or clap it all together.

Step 3: Make a rhythm that fills in the spaces the primary rhythm creates. Clap or play that rhythm together.

> *Tip: Don't worry about harmony when first trying this exercise. Focus on the rhythm, and enjoy the crunch of random intervals!*
>
> *If you want to add in harmonic considerations, do it as a separate exercise, after everyone is comfortable rhythmically.*

Step 4: Half of the group play the primary rhythm, the other half play the rhythm of the spaces in it.

Step 5: While the rest of the group plays the primary rhythm, each person takes a turn improvising a second part that accents a part of the primary rhythm.

Step 6: While the rest of the group plays the primary rhythm, each person takes a turn improvising a second part that occurs in the spaces within the primary rhythm.

Step 7: While the rest of the group plays the primary rhythm, each person takes a turn improvising a second part, with no restrictions.

Exercise 33: Awareness 2

Step 1: Improvise a group groove with everyone playing.

Step 2: While continuing to play, direct your attention to what everyone else is playing, focusing on one person at a time. Use this focus as an opportunity to sync up your part with each of the other player's parts.

Step 3: Still continuing to play, direct your attention back to hearing all parts simultaneously. Focus on how all the parts (including your own) fit together into one groove.

Step 4: Continue to play the groove for long enough to allow this new awareness of your relationship with the other parts to deepen it, then end.

Exercise 34: Take It to the Bridge 1

Step 1: Count off a tempo. Improvise a group groove.

Step 2: Allow time for the groove to settle into place.

Step 3: Once the first groove is locked in anyone can change what they are doing. This is the signal for everyone to change.

Step 4: Allow the new groove to settle in.

Step 5: Someone change back to the part they played in the initial groove. This is the signal for everyone to change back to their parts from that groove.

Exercise 35: Playing Over a Groove 1

Step 1: Improvise a group groove.

Step 2: Allow time for everyone to settle into the groove.

Step 3: One person stops playing their part of the groove, then comes back in, improvising whatever they want over the groove.

Tip: If you are having trouble hearing when someone changes parts or remembering your parts from the first groove, do Exercise 33: Awareness 2.

Step 4: Repeat Step 3 until everyone has had a turn improvising over the groove.

Exercise 36: Playing Over a Groove 2

Step 1: Improvise a group groove.

Step 2: Allow time for everyone to settle into the groove.

Step 3: One person stops playing their part of the groove, comes back in improvising a melody, then returns to their original part.

Step 4: Repeat Step 3 until everyone has had a turn improvising a melody over the groove.

Tip: Here are three things that will make what you play sound like a melody rather than another part of the groove: 1) The phrases of your melodic statement are longer than the length of the groove (for example, the groove is two bars repeating, your melody is eight bars) 2) You leave space for your melody to breathe between repetitions. 3) Your melody is louder or more prominent than the groove (this often means everyone else has to get softer). For more on understanding and playing melodies, see Exercises 83-91.

Exercise 37: Playing Over a Groove 3

Step 1: Improvise a group groove.

Step 2: Allow time for everyone to settle into the groove.

Step 3: One person stops playing their part of the groove, then improvises a melody, a solo, and the same melody again.

Step 4: The person who has improvised over the groove is responsible for cueing the ending. (For more on ending grooves, see Exercises 40-41.)

Exercise 38: Playing Over Two Grooves

Step 1: Improvise a group groove.

Step 2: Allow time for the groove to settle into place. This is Groove A.

Step 3: Once the first groove is locked in, anyone can change what they are doing. This is the signal for everyone to change.

Step 4: Allow the new groove to settle in. This is Groove B.

Step 5: On cue, switch back to Groove A (this can be a vocal cue, a physical motion, or someone changing to their part in Groove A).

Step 6: One person drops out of the groove and plays a melody or other improvisation on Groove A.

Step 7: The end of their improvisation is the cue for Groove B. Another soloist improvises over Groove B.

Step 8: Go back and forth between the two sections as much as you like, with a different soloist over each section.

Step 9: The last soloist cues the ending.

Exercise 39: Role Playing

It is essential to be aware of the role each part plays and how it functions in the groove. A groove improvisation is most clear when everyone understands the roles chosen by everyone else and can hear when anyone changes to a different part or role.

The parts we choose to play in a groove often reflect common roles used in the groove music we are familiar with (the examples I give are common roles in R&B music). It's useful to practice recognizing common role choices, both in order to learn how to function in whatever role we choose, and to be able to experiment with creating grooves that do not conform to common sets of roles.

Step 1: Improvise a group groove.

Step 2: Pay attention to the role choices that have been made, and how they function in the groove. (Who has chosen to play bass lines? Rhythmic accompaniment similar to the comping of a guitar or piano player? Who's chosen to play melodic lines? Horn type riffs? Rhythmic accents or drum beats? Melodic lines?) It's not important that you name them, but it is important that you hear them.

Step 3: Stay in your chosen role throughout the improvisation.

Step 4: Improvise another groove, but this time consciously choose a different role. If certain roles are not being filled or if the same players are constantly migrating to the same roles, you can decide in advance who is going to have what role.

Exercise 40: Ending a Groove

Unlike other kinds of improvising, there is rarely an obvious natural ending to a groove. By its very nature, a groove wants to continue indefinitely, so an ending must somehow be created. The next two exercises will give you practice in some of the common ways of creating endings for grooves.

Step 1: Improvise a group groove.

Step 2: Practice ending this groove in the different ways outlined in Steps 3-6. Start the groove again and end again, until you have tried all the different methods.

Tip: Make sure you have everyone's attention before you cue the ending.

Experiment with stopping the groove at different points. Your cue will work better if it comes at a natural ending place in the phrasing of the groove.

Step 3: Gradually slow down the groove, until the momentum stops and it ends.

Step 4: Fade out the groove by getting softer and softer until you can no longer hear it and it ends.

Step 5: Let the groove end by dissolving/morphing into a short textural section. (see Exercise 52: Improvising a Texture)

Step 6: Have each member of the group practice cueing an abrupt stop.

Exercise 41: Ending on a Riff

At least one part in every groove (usually several) can be used as an ending "riff", a line the players can gravitate to that sounds like a natural ending point.

Step 1: Improvise a group groove.

Step 2: Identify the parts in the groove that could be used as an ending riff.

Tip: One of the wonderful things about free improvisation is that any instrument can play any role, not just those roles traditionally assigned to it. Take advantage of this by learning how to function in both traditional and nontraditional roles.

Step 3: Try ending on each part, by having some of the players gravitate to that part and repeat it until an ending is cued.

> *Tip: Enough people have to play the ending riff to make it a prominent part of the overall musical fabric. See Exercise 50-51 for practice in gravitating to a particular line.*
>
> *If you are having trouble identifying which parts are potential ending riffs, try ending on different places in each part. See which sounds like a natural ending.*
>
> *Many of these ending choices can also be used as a way of beginning a groove.*

Varying the Groove

Have you ever been in a room when an air conditioner or heater turns on? At first the sound is very noticeable, but after a short time you get used to it. It becomes a part of the background noise and you no longer pay much attention to it, until it turns off again. The same thing happens with a groove – if it stays the same for too long it stops commanding attention. Varying the groove helps keep it interesting, but if you vary it too much it will sound like you are playing a different groove. The following exercises deal with some ways to create variation while still keeping the essential character of the original groove.

Exercise 42: Awareness 3

Step 1: Improvise a group groove.

Step 2: While continuing to play, direct your attention one by one to what everyone else is playing, then to all parts simultaneously.

Step 3: On cue, switch from the part you are playing to someone else's part. One person can be assigned to cue, or the first person who changes parts can be the cue for everyone to change.

Step 4: On cue, switch back to your original part.

Exercise 43: Varying Your Part

Step 1: Improvise a group groove.

Step 2: Instead of trying to keep your part the same, experiment with how to vary your part while still keeping the basic sound and feel of the groove.

> *Tip: Some notes in each part are more important to the feel of the groove than others. These are often the notes that are most accented and/or the most important melodically. Experiment with slowly taking out the least important notes until you are down to a few essential notes or rhythms, then adding back in around them. Play each variation of your part enough times that you can get a good feel for how it works and everyone else can have a chance to hear and respond to it.*

Exercise 44: Break It Down 1

Another common way to vary a groove is to vary the intensity, by bringing it down and building it back up again. One way to do this is by using dynamics (how loud or soft it is).

Step 1: Improvise a group groove.

Step 2: On cue, suddenly get softer then gradually build the volume back up. Do this until you are comfortable changing dynamics together.

Exercise 45: Break It Down 2

Step 1: Improvise a group groove.

Step 2: Take turns being in the lead role by playing a melody or solo over the groove. At every change of lead, bring the dynamics down, then let them naturally get softer or louder with whatever the lead player is playing.

Exercise 46: Break It Down 3

You can also vary a groove by changing the people playing it. Subtracting players tends to bring the volume and intensity down, adding them back in tends to build it up. Different combinations of players also give the groove a different feeling, even when they are playing the same basic parts.

Step 1: Improvise a group groove.

Step 2: On cue, break down into a smaller group. You can say what this smaller group will be ahead of time or you can improvise it in the moment.

Step 3: Add the other players back in, either singly or in groups.

Step 4: On cue, break down into a different smaller group, then build back up again. Continue until everyone has had an opportunity to play in one of the smaller groups.

Exercise 47: Break It Down 4

Step 1: Improvise a group groove.

Step 2: Take turns being in the lead role, playing over the groove. At every change of lead, break down into a smaller group, then build by adding players back in.

Tip: Everything in every part of the groove is material that is available for you to use.

Experiment with all different sizes and makeup of groups. Use all different combinations of instruments. See Exercises 75-82 for further exploration of Groups Within the Group.

When adding back in, remember you can choose to play with an already existing part (see Exercises 48-49).

> **Tip:** *Awareness of the space in a groove is essential. If too much is happening in any particular sonic space, the groove can become cluttered and sound muddy. This does not only apply to rhythmic space. It is just as true of other kinds of sonic space, such as dynamics, timbre, and pitch range. A cluttered and chaotic feel can be an interesting effect when used intentionally, but it is just one of the many possible feels a groove can have.*

Joining With an Already Existing Part

When adding a part to an improvised groove you must choose whether you are going to play with what someone else is playing, in some of the spaces left by them, or some combination of the two. This series of exercises gives you practice in choosing to play with them.

Exercise 48: Playing With 1

Step 1: One player begins the groove with an ostinato pattern.

Step 2: The second player has the choice to play with the first person's line or to play something else.

Step 3: If the second player chooses to play with the first person's line, the third player can choose to play with them or play something else. If the second player has chosen to play something else, the third player must play with either already existing part.

Step 4: If the third player has chosen to play with another part, the fourth player can make either choice. If the third player has chosen to play something else, the fourth player must play with one of the other existing lines.

Step 5: Continue in a similar manner until all players are locked into a groove, then end.

> ***Tip:*** *"Playing with" someone else does not necessarily mean playing the exact same thing as them. Anything that has the effect of emphasizing their line or a part of their line instead of taking up a different space will have the desired result (for example, play all or part of the line in unison, play a harmony part to some or all of the line, add rhythmic accents to parts of the line).*

Exercise 49: Playing With 2

Step 1: Divide the group into two. Pair each person in the group with someone else.

Step 2: Improvise a group groove. The players in each pair play with each other, coming to agreement as quickly as possible on their mutual line, and stay together throughout the improvisation.

Exercise 50: Coming Together 1

Step 1: Improvise a group groove.

Step 2: Everyone gradually gravitate to playing one thing together.

Exercise 51: Coming Together 2

Step 1: Improvise a group groove, with everyone starting at the same time.

Step 2: As quickly as possible, gravitate to playing one thing together.

> ***Tip:*** *This is good practice in being strong, yet flexible. In order for it to work, you must come in with your strongest idea, yet be willing to instantly go to whatever becomes the consensus. Don't focus on playing the same thing, focus on moving to the same place.*

SEVEN

Textures

At any moment in time, any place in the world has a unique sonic landscape (soundscape). Not only does a beach sound different from a city street, each particular beach sounds different from every other beach, and any moment at that beach has its own unique set of sounds.

A musical texture is a soundscape created by a particular group of people at a particular time. These textures can in themselves be the focus of an improvisation or they can serve as a background for people to play over, like a person walking through a landscape.

Tip: Although they may initially seem very different, a groove and a texture are closely related improvisationally. A groove is a specific kind of texture in time. When a texture is repeated in a consciously rhythmic way, it becomes a groove.

Any group of sounds, when played together and repeated, create their own unique musical texture. There is no limit to the kinds of textures that can be created in this way.

Exercise 52: Improvising a Texture
Step 1: Take a moment to be still and listen to the sounds around and within you.

Step 2: Wait for an impulse to movement. Allow that impulse to create sound. Whatever happens, stay with that material for the entire improvisation.

Tip: Notice how these textures tend to repeat at a specific interval, to naturally "breathe" in a similar way. Experiment with both allowing that phrasing to establish itself and with consciously varying it.

Step 3: Once everyone who wants to play is playing, this group of sounds is the group's texture of this moment. Improvise with this texture until satisfied, then end.

Exercise 53: Lots of Textures
Step 1: Improvise a lot of textures in a row, with short pauses in between. Play each texture just long enough to establish its character before going on to the next one. Try to make each one different from the last.

Exercise 54: Take It to the Bridge 2

Step 1: Improvise a group texture.

Step 2: Allow time for the texture to establish itself.

Tip: For different effects, practice changing between textures both gradually and suddenly.

Step 3: Once the first texture is established, anyone can change what they are doing. This is the signal for everyone to change.

Step 4: Allow the new texture to settle in.

Step 5: Someone change back to the part they played in the initial texture. This is the signal for everyone to change back to their parts from that texture.

Exercise 55: Playing Over a Texture 1

Step 1: Improvise a group texture.

Step 2: Allow time for the texture to establish itself.

Step 3: One person stops playing their part of the texture, then comes back in, improvising whatever they want over the texture.

Step 4: Repeat Step 3 until everyone has had a turn improvising.

Exercise 56: Playing Over a Texture 2

Step 1: Improvise a group texture.

Step 2: Allow time for the texture to establish itself.

Step 3: One person stops playing their part of the texture, then comes back in improvising a melody.

Tip: In this context, melody does not necessarily mean a series of notes. The melody can be any sound or series of sounds that takes the lead role or occupies the sonic and psychic space that a melody would traditionally occupy.

Step 4: Repeat Step 3 until everyone has had a turn improvising a melody over the texture.

Exercise 57: Playing Over Two Textures

Step 1: Improvise a group texture.

Step 2: Allow time for the texture to establish itself. This is Texture A.

Step 3: Once the first texture is established anyone can change what they are doing. This is the signal for everyone to change.

Step 4: Allow the new texture to establish itself. This is Texture B.

Step 5: On cue, switch back to Texture A (this can be a vocal cue, a physical cue, or someone changing to their part in A).

Step 6: One person drops out of the texture and plays a melody or other improvisation on Texture A.

Step 7: The end of their improvisation is the cue for Texture B. Another person improvises over Texture B.

Step 8: Go back and forth between the two sections as much as you like, with a different soloist over each section.

Step 9: The last soloist cues the ending.

Exercise 58: Awareness 4

Because of our basic personality and life experience, each of us has certain tendencies that affect how we approach and interact with other people. These same tendencies affect how we improvise music with them. Some people like to enter a new situation cautiously while others barge in recklessly. Some people's first reaction is to want to play with what others are playing and some instinctively play in opposition to them. Awareness of your personal tendencies will help you to improvise out of choice rather than habit.

Step 1: For the rest of the practice session, include in your awareness how you tend to react and what kind of role you most often choose to play in the group dynamics.

Step 2: At the end of the session discuss this among yourselves. Do the other people in the group agree or disagree with your assessment? What did you notice about the tendencies of others in the group?

Step 3: Keep this awareness in mind in later sessions. For some of the exercises in that session consciously choose a different kind of reaction and/or role.

Tip: Sometimes a simple awareness of your tendencies is enough to make them no longer habitual. Sometimes awareness is not enough. Acting in other ways feels uncomfortable or just plain wrong, and you must consciously practice acting differently in order to allow yourself to experience and feel comfortable with different kinds of improvisatory relationships.

Varying Textures

Improvised textures are generally less specific and rhythmically static than improvised grooves, but learning how to create variation without losing the sound and feel of the original texture is still very useful. It allows you to create improvisations of all different shapes, to give a sense of tension and release, and to sustain interest over the course of a long or multi-section improvisation.

Exercise 59: Varying Dynamics in a Texture 1

One way to change a texture is to vary its dynamics.

Step 1: Improvise a group texture.

Step 2: Practice making the texture louder and softer. Do this until you are comfortable changing dynamics together.

Tip: Practice changing dynamics both gradually and suddenly. Try varying the relative volume of the different parts. Notice how that changes the sound and feel of the texture.

Exercise 60: Varying Dynamics in a Texture 2

Step 1: Improvise a group texture.

Step 2: Take turns being in the lead role, playing a melody or solo over the texture. The people who are playing the texture focus on supporting the soloist by changing dynamics in response to the dynamics of the solo.

Tip: Changing dynamics with the soloist is the traditional choice of dynamic relationship between soloist and accompaniment. What other choices are there? How do they affect the music?

Exercise 61: Varying Density in a Texture 1

Another way to vary a texture is by increasing and decreasing its density. Textural density has two different aspects: the ratio of silence to sound, and the amount of sound happening at any particular time. Playing with these two aspects allows considerable variation without changing the essential elements of the texture. This exercise practices changing the ratio of silence and sound.

Step 1: Improvise a group texture.

Step 2: While playing the same texture, increase the amount of time you are playing silence and decrease the amount of time you are playing sound.

Step 3: When you feel like the improvisation is about to collapse from inertia, start increasing the density again by increasing the amount of time you are playing sound and decreasing the amount of time you are playing silence.

Step 4: When you feel like the improvisation is about to explode into chaos, decrease the density again until you get back to the silence to sound ratio the texture had in Step 1.

Exercise 62: Varying Density in a Texture 2

Step 1: Improvise a group texture.

Step 2: Gradually move your part in the texture to the same space as other people's parts until you have areas of very dense texture separated by areas of silence.

Step 3: Gradually move your part back to its original relationship to the other parts in the texture.

Exercise 63: Break It Down 5

You can create variation by breaking down into smaller groups and improvising with different parts of the whole texture.

Step 1: Improvise a group texture.

Step 2: After the texture is well established, some players drop out. The remaining players improvise a new section of the improvisation using the material of the remaining parts of the texture.

Step 3: Add the other players back in, reestablishing the original texture.

Step 4: Repeat Steps 2 and 3 as much as you want, exploring different aspects of the original texture.

Exercise 64: Playing Within a Texture

You can choose to play your own individual part in a group texture or you can choose to play with someone else. This basic choice is the same one you make when improvising a groove together, but the nature of textural improvisation makes the concept of *playing together* a bit more abstract.

Step 1: Each player chooses one other player they are going to play with, without telling the others.

Step 2: Improvise a group texture.

Step 3: Each player plays with the player they have chosen. Continue playing with them until the end of the improvisation.

Exercise 65: Moving to Each Part

Step 1: Improvise a group texture.

Step 2: Everyone gravitate to playing one part of the texture together.

Step 3: Go back to your original part.

Step 4: Repeat Steps 2 and 3 until you have played each part of the texture together, then end.

Tip: You can play together in the same sense as in Exercise 12: Mirroring, where you are trying to play the same thing at the same time. You can also "play with" by choosing to play the same kind of sound or gesture as someone else.

EIGHT

Creating Space – Playing Silence

Music is both sound and silence. We tend to think of improvising as playing a series of sounds, but it is the silence and space between these sounds that define them. The first and most important choice in any group improvisation is whether to play sound or play silence.

The exercises in this section are designed to help develop an awareness of the importance of silence and avoid the common problem of everyone playing sound all the time.

Exercise 66: Silence and Sound
Step 1: Play an improvisation. Everyone must play silence for as much time as they play sound. You can structure your sound and silence however you want, but by the end of the improvisation they should have been of similar duration.

Exercise 67: Together
Step 1: Play an improvisation where everyone starts and ends phrases at the same time.

Exercise 68: Apart
Step 1: Play an improvisation where no one is supposed to play at the same time as anyone else.

Exercise 69: Together Blind
Step 1: Play an improvisation where everyone starts and ends phrases at the same time, with your eyes closed.

Exercise 70: Apart Blind
Step 1: Play an improvisation where no one is supposed to play at the same time as anyone else, with your eyes closed.

Exercise 71: Together and Apart 1
Step 1: Play an improvisation that goes back and forth between playing together and playing separately.

Exercise 72: Together and Apart 2

Step 1: Play an improvisation where no one is supposed to play at the same time as anyone else.

Step 2: If two people play at the same time, they must immediately play a duet together.

Step 3: When the duet is over everyone else comes back in, still trying not to play at the same time.

Step 4: Repeat Steps 2 and 3 until the improvisation ends.

Exercise 73: Together and Apart 3

Step 1: Play an improvisation where no one is supposed to play at the same time as anyone else.

Step 2: Any people that play at the same time must then play together for the rest of the improvisation.

Step 3: Continue until everyone is playing together.

Exercise 74: Wanting to Play

Step 1: Get ready to play.

Step 2: Watch your impulse to create a sound, but don't actually play until you have to play, until you can't stand it anymore, until you absolutely *need* to play.

Step 3: When you no longer feel that need to play, stop playing. Don't come back in until you feel that passionate need to play.

Tip: Trust that you will get a chance to play. Trust that if you are not playing those that are will play beautifully, and at some point the music will ask you to play again.

NINE

Groups Within the Group

Every group of players contains within it the possibilities of many different combinations, of different groups within the group. The bigger the group is, the more combinations there are (i.e., a quartet contains within it 4 different solos, 6 different duos, 4 different trios and 1 quartet). These exercises explore the improvisational possibilities of using these different groups within the group.

Exercise 75: Groups Within the Group 1
Step 1: Player 1 and Player 2 play a duet.

Step 2: Player 3 comes in and Player 1 drops out. Player 2 and Player 3 play a duet.

Step 3: Player 4 comes in and Player 2 drops out. Player 3 and Player 4 play a duet. Continue around the circle in this way until you are done.

Exercise 76: Groups Within the Group 2
Step 1: Play an improvisation where only two people can be playing at the same time. If a third person comes in, one person has to drop out. If two people come in at once, both players have to drop out.

Step 2: Play Step 1 again, except this time have three people playing at once (if your group is larger than three), or four people playing at once (if your group is larger than four).

Tip: Experiment with varying the pace of these changes between different groups. It gives a very different effect if you go very quickly between different groups or if you let each group's section of the piece have its own space for development. The former is in itself an improvisational strategy. The latter provides opportunities for a large variety of improvised forms and structures.

Don't force it! Use the natural ending points that occur in the improvisation as an opportunity to change groups.

Exercise 77: Groups Within the Group 3

Step 1: Play an improvisation. At some point in the improvisation someone will play an unaccompanied solo. You can leave this open or assign who will be the soloist.

Step 2: Play as in Step 1, but break down to a duo or trio instead of an unaccompanied solo.

Exercise 78: Groups Within the Group 4

Step 1: Play an improvisation. Alternate group improvisation with unaccompanied solo, until everyone has had a chance to play an unaccompanied solo.

Step 2: Play as in Step 1, but break down to duos or trios instead of unaccompanied solos.

Exercise 79: Groups Within the Group 5

Step 1: Create a form to improvise within, based on the number of people playing in each section, like full group-solo-duet-trio-full group, or solo-full group-trio-full-group-solo.

Exercise 80: Groups Within the Group 6

Step 1: Play a multipart improvisation where you leave the form of the improvisation open, but stipulate what size groups will occur during it. For example, you could decide that at some point in the improvisation there would be a solo, a duo, and a trio.

Exercise 81: Groups Within the Group 7

Step 1: Play a multipart improvisation with the goal of breaking down into at least one smaller group at some point during the improvisation.

Exercise 82: Groups Within the Group 8

There can also be different size groups within the group playing at the same time.

Step 1: Split the group up into several smaller groups.

Step 2: Play an improvisation where the players stay in these groups throughout, whether everyone is playing all together or just the people in one particular group are playing.

TEN

Melody and Accompaniment

Melody and accompaniment is a very familiar musical relationship. We've heard it our whole lives. We instinctively know what a melody is, and how it functions. We hear where it begins and ends. We know immediately what is the lead voice and what is the background to that voice. This innately understood relationship is a powerful improvisational tool.

In free improvisation almost any series of sounds can function as melody or accompaniment. Even though we are not relying on traditional boundaries to define what is melody and what is accompaniment, there are many unconscious clues that can cause us to hear something as foreground or as background.

Exercise 83: A Simple Melody
Step 1: One player slowly makes up a melodic line, note by note, while everyone else follows them. After the melody is complete, play it together, with the creator of the melody cueing the rhythm.

Step 2: Take turns doing this until everyone has had a turn creating a melody.

Exercise 84: Melody and Accompaniment 1
Step 1: One person improvises a melody, the other two improvise accompaniment.

Step 2: The melody person plays the same melody again, and the accompanists explore different ways to accompany it.

Exercise 85: Melody and Accompaniment 2
Step 1: Improvise a background (this can be any number of players, and any kind of background).

Step 2: One person improvises a melody over this background, leaves some space, then repeats the same melody.

Tip: A melody can be thought of as the narrative voice of an improvisation, telling the story and providing a sense of coherence through the cycles of tension and release. The accompaniment is the background this narrator is moving through. Both have equal power to affect the overall feeling of an improvisation. The same person walking through a sunlit meadow or on the edge of a cliff gives very different feelings.

Tip: Playing the melodies of the other players in your group gives you an understanding of the kinds of melodies they hear. An awareness of each other's personal melodic language greatly enhances the group's ability to improvise together.

Step 3: Repeat Step 2 until everyone has had a chance to improvise a melody.

Step 4: If you want more practice improvising backgrounds as a group, play each melody numerous times, with a different background each time or change backgrounds for each person's melody.

Exercise 86: Melody and Accompaniment 3

Being able to remember and repeat a melody you have created allows you to improvise with it.

Step 1: One person improvises a melody, the other two improvise accompaniment.

Step 2: Play an improvisation using both this melody and accompaniment as the materials for the improvisation.

Step 3: End the improvisation by playing the original statement of melody and accompaniment again.

Tip: If you hear your melody start to wander, lose track of it, or can't remember it, stop playing. Try to repeat it from the beginning. The part you remember is most likely the initial impulse, the seed of your melody. It may be as small as an interval, a rhythm, or a few notes together that form a short phrase. You may be surprised how simple this initial melodic impulse is, but don't try to turn it into something else. Just let it be what it is: a simple beautiful melody. What you're learning is how to hear that first seed of inspiration and hold onto it long enough to let a simple melody flow from it. Once you learn how to do this try to create more complex melodies and forms, by improvising different variations and developments of the initial impulse, and by adding to it.

Exercise 87: Melody and Accompaniment 4

Step 1: Improvise a background (this can be any number of players).

Step 2: One person improvises a melody over this background, improvises a solo or variations of the melodic material, then repeats the same melody.

Step 3: Repeat Steps 1 and 2 until everyone has had a chance in the lead role.

Exercise 88: Improvising With Melody

Step 1: Pick or create a simple melody everyone knows or can learn easily, like a nursery rhyme or children's song.

Step 2: Play the melody together in every way you can think of, as in Steps 3-14.

Step 3: Play it in unison (in and out of time).

Step 4: Play it as a canon (a simple canon is a round, like Row, Row, Row Your Boat).

Tip: Anything can be a background, as long as it doesn't eclipse the melody as the focus of attention. You can use grooves (see Chapter 6) or textural backgrounds (see Chapter 7) or a combination of the two.

The improvisation can begin with the accompaniment, the person improvising the melody, or both can start at once. Try it all three ways.

Step 5: Everyone start at the same time but play it in their own way.

Step 6: Use the notes of the melody but change the rhythms.

Step 7: Use the rhythms but change the notes.

Step 8: Have someone conduct it.

Step 9: Improvise a piece using only the notes and rhythms of the melody.

Step 10: One or more people play the melody while others in the group improvise textural accompaniments to the melody.

Step 11: Improvise group grooves and play the melody on top of them.

Step 12: Improvise a harmony to the melody.

Step 13: Improvise a counterpoint to the melody.

Step 14: Play the melody as an accompaniment (try it at different speeds, and with different instruments). Improvise over it!

Exercise 89: Group Melody

Step 1: One at a time, each person plays four notes while the others follow them.

Step 2: Play these 4 note phrases as one long melody.

Step 3: Play these 4 note phrases as a series of 4 note chords.

Step 4: Play improvisations with the group melody as motivic material.

Step 5: Have each person create their own rhythms for the notes of this group melody, then have the group imitate their rhythm.

Step 6: Play each 4 note chord in sequence as a background for improvising.

Step 7: Number each 4 note chord and have someone conduct them in whatever order they wish, then have people improvise over them.

Step 8: Improvise a groove or grooves out of the group melody, or the 4 note chords from the melody, or different parts of the melody. Then play the entire melody over it, or improvise over it.

Exercise 90: Awareness 5

Step 1: Everyone except one person hold out a note.

Step 2: One person plays a short melody and repeats it a few times.

Step 3: Everyone else plays or sings that melody.

Exercise 91: Melody With a Second Person

Step 1: Part of the group improvises an accompaniment or background.

Step 2: One person improvises a melody, playing it through two times. The second time they play through the melody another person plays it with them, either in unison, harmony, or counterpoint.

Step 3: Improvise more with this material and repeat the melody again at the end.

ELEVEN

Musical Parameters

Improvisational exercises can be used to explore any musical parameter or combination of parameters, simply by making them the subject of an improvisation.

Exercise 92: Dynamics

Step 1: Play an improvisation, saying beforehand what the dynamic shape will be. Try as many as you can think of and see what effect it has on the overall improvisation. You can create dynamics by each person playing louder or softer, or by adding and subtracting players.

Tip: In addition to the traditional dynamics notation, you can draw any kind of graphic representation of the overall dynamic shape of the improvisation. At this point you are starting to experiment with graphic notation, as in Exercise 97: Visual Stimuli.

For example:
Play an improvisation with this dynamic shape < >

Or this one < < <

Or this one > <

Exercise 93: Opposites

There are many parameters that can be seen as being on a scale that goes from one extreme to another (for instance, dynamics is a scale with soft at one end and loud at the other). Playing improvisations that explore these kinds of opposite extremes is a good way to explore the parameters involved.

Step 1: Choose a pair of musical opposites based on a musical parameter, like rhythm (fast/slow), pitch (high/low), articulation (staccato/legato), use of space (sparse/dense), etc.

Step 2: Play an improvisation where all players explore one of the pair of extremes.

Step 3: Play an improvisation where all players explore both of the extremes.

Step 4: Play an improvisation where each player chooses one of the extremes to explore.

Exercise 94: Form

If the group wishes to improvise longer forms, each member of the group must be able to recognize when different sections occur, and must be able to remember and return to previously improvised sections. You have already been improvising on forms in some of the previous exercises, but this exercise gives you focused practice in being able to recognize different sections of an improvisation and return to them at will.

Tip: Conscious exploration of larger forms creates a group awareness of structure. This makes it possible to improvise compositionally and avoid having every improvisation be a series of different sections (ABCDE , etc.)

Step 1: Play an improvisation where you agree on the form in advance (for example AB, ABA, ABACA, where each letter is a different section). When you go back to the same section again, it can be the same, a variation, or a development of the original section.

Exercise 95: Scales

You can do improvisational exercises with the instruction that the notes used must be from a particular scale (a group of notes ascending or descending in fixed intervals).

Tip: You can do this as a separate exercise, or as an added instruction to any other improvisation exercise.

Step 1: You can make up your own group scale by having each person choose a note, going up or down until you reach an octave, or you can use a scale you already know.

Step 2: Play an improvisation using that scale.

Step 3: Once the group is comfortable sticking to a scale, play an improvisation where the scale is a "home base" that you can go away from and come back to.

TWELVE

Tasting Shapes

Anything can be used as inspiration for musical improvisation.

Exercise 96: Emotions
Step 1: Name an emotion, then play it.

Exercise 97: Visual Stimuli
Step 1: Play a piece of visual art, a photograph, the scene outside your window. Create your own visual representation (graphic notation) and play it. What do the different colors sound like? Use the graphics in this book as the subject of improvisation!

Exercise 98: Words 1
Step 1: Play an improvisation as accompaniment to a poem or story as it is being recited.

Exercise 99: Words 2
Step 1: Pick any word, phrase, or short story. Read it, then play it.

Tip: If you are having trouble thinking of something to play, pick up any newspaper, magazine or book and grab an interesting phrase or short descriptive story from it.

Exercise 100: Movement 1
Everything moves through time and space, just as music does.

Step 1: Play any movement – a leaf drifting down, the wind blowing through a tree, the movement of people, animals and vehicles outside your window.

Exercise 101: Movement 2
Step 1: Have each member of the group move around however they like, while the others in the group play their movement.

Tip: Your whole body improvises music, not just your fingers and your instrument. Your improvisation is not just the sounds you create, it is the way you are in this particular moment. The music is much more powerful if your physical expression and musical expression have the same intention, so be aware of how you are standing or sitting, and what messages your body and physical attitude are sending.

Exercise 102: Movement 3

Step 1: Move to each other's playing. If you have an instrument that allows you to do so, walk around and move while playing.

Exercise 103: The Sounds Around Us

Step 1: There is sound everywhere, all the time. Stay silent and listen, then base your improvisation on what you hear, or improvise with the sounds you are hearing.

Exercise 104: Conducting

Step 1: Take turns being the conductor, conducting the group's improvisation using physical gestures and/or words.

THIRTEEN

Combining Exercises

As you become more familiar with using improvisational exercises, experiment with combining them. You can add more instructions to create a more complex exercise, string together different exercises to create longer forms, or a combination of both. There are innumerable ways to do this, depending on the interests of your group.

Exercise 105: Group Groove + Group Texture

This exercise combines creating grooves, creating textures, and playing them in an ABAB form. You can do this exercise with any form you choose, by simply adding more sections.

Tip: You can also do this exercise with two grooves or two textures. When using two grooves, experiment with making them both the same tempo and time signature and with making them different.

Step 1: Split the group into two subgroups.

Step 2: Group 1 improvises a group groove.

Step 3: On cue, Group 2 comes in improvising a group texture. Group 1 either fades out or stops.

Tip: Remember to create variation in both the groove and textural accompaniment, so every section does not sound the same (see Exercises 42-47 and 59-65).

Step 4: Go back and forth between the two. When Group 1 is playing, players from Group 2 solo over the groove. When Group 2 is playing, players from Group 1 solo over the texture.

Step 5: End with both groups playing at the same time.

Exercise 106: Solos + Conducted Group Interludes

Step 1: Each person in the group improvises a solo, with conducted group interludes in between. It's fun to have the soloist also be the conductor for the interlude that comes before or after their solo.

Step 2: Do the same exercise, but use duos or trios in the place of solos.

Exercise 107: Short Textures + Dynamics

Step 1: Play a number of short textures, but instead of leaving space between them, make each texture a dynamic shape, like < > (changing textures at the loudest point) or > < (changing textures at the softest point).

Exercise 108: Form + Anything

Step 1: Decide on a form for your improvisation (see Exercise 94: Form).

Step 2: Further define some or all of the sections by adding another instruction to them, from any of the previous exercises in the book.

Step 3: Play an improvisation based on these instructions.

FOURTEEN

Warm-Ups

Tip: If the group is getting too self-conscious or overly serious, put down your instruments and do some theatre exercises, then bring that sense of fun back into your music improvisation work. Often simply screaming, making weird noises, or jumping around in a crazy way as a group, will loosen things up and bring back a sense of fun and playfulness. This will also help clear your mind between exercises if you get a particular tempo, feel, or song stuck in your head.

It's useful to play at least one warm-up exercise before beginning an improvisation session. In this chapter I have written out some of the warm-ups I use most often, although almost any fairly simple exercise will work. I often use theatre improvisation warm-ups, as they provide a nice transition from the more usual mediums of improvisation (voice and movement) to intensive work on musical improvisation.

Exercise 109: Say Hello
Each person plays a short solo improvisation. It's a good way to say hello.

Exercise 110: Sound Ball 1
Step 1: Imagine every sound is a physical object that you can throw.

Tip: Particularly in the early stages of learning to improvise, playing a short solo is a great way to practice being in the moment and telling the truth.

Step 2: One person makes a sound, then throws it to the next person in the circle.

Step 3: That person catches the sound, transforms it however they wish, and throws it to the next person in the circle.

Step 4: Continue until you want to stop.

Exercise 111: Sound Ball 2

Step 1: Imagine every sound is a physical object that you can throw.

Step 2: One person makes a sound, then throws it to anyone else in the group.

Step 3: That person catches the sound, transforms it however they wish, and throws it to someone else.

Tip: How do you get someone to understand you are throwing the sound to them? Exploring that question will greatly enhance the group's cueing and nonverbal communication while playing.

Step 4: Continue until you want to stop.

Exercise 112: Sound Ball 3

Step 1: Imagine every sound is a physical object that you can throw. Use a simple adjective to describe the sound ball or how it behaves (hot, spiky, floating, etc.).

Step 2: One person makes a sound, then throws it to whomever they wish, taking into account the description of the ball.

Step 3: That person catches the sound, transforms it, and throws it to someone else.

Step 4: Continue until you want to stop.

Exercise 113: Human Machine

This is like the basic group groove exercise, except done with voice and physical motion. It is a good warm-up for practicing groove improvisation.

Tip: This is most fun when the movements physically interact with each other, like the cogs and pistons of a machine.

Step 1: One person makes a repetitive rhythmic sound and motion.

Step 2: Each person adds their own sound and motion, until everyone is moving and sounding together.

Exercise 114: Free Association

This exercise is done while standing in a circle, without instruments.

Step 1: Count off a tempo. On each beat, a person says a word in sequence around the circle. It doesn't matter what the word is, as long as the rhythm isn't broken. Say whatever word first comes to mind. Make up a default word, like banana, for everyone to say if they can't think of a word.

Exercise 115: Digits

This exercise is done while standing in a circle, without instruments. The object of the game is to count from one to ten as a group.

Tip: Exercise 115: Digits is a good warm-up for Exercises 67-73.

Step 1: Any player starts by saying "one".
Any other player can say "two", and so on. If more than one player says a number at the same time you must start back at "one" again.

Exercise 116: Monkey See, Monkey Do 1

This exercise is done while standing in a circle, without instruments.

Step 1: One person steps into the center of the circle and makes a sound and/or gesture.

Step 2: Everyone else imitates them, and keeps repeating the sound and/or gesture.

Step 3: The person in the center moves to someone else's place in the circle. That person then moves to the center and does their own sound and/or gesture.

Step 4: Everyone else imitates the new sound/gesture.

Step 5: Continue this sequence for as long as you wish.

Exercise 117: Monkey See, Monkey Do 2

This exercise is done while standing in a circle, without instruments.

Step 1: One person steps into the center of the circle and makes a sound and/or gesture.

Step 2: Everyone else imitates them, then keeps repeating the sound and/or gesture while gradually exaggerating it. Make it bigger and bigger until it's as big as it could possibly be, then make it smaller and smaller until it's as small as it could possibly be.

Step 3: The person in the center moves to someone else's place in the circle. That person then moves to the center and does their own sound and/or gesture. Continue for as long as it's fun.

Exercise 118: Naming Things Wrong

Everyone walks around the room at the same time, examining the objects in it. As each object is examined name it out loud, but give it a different name than usual.

Exercise 119: Awareness 6

Step 1: Stand or sit in a relaxed, ready to play position.

Step 2: Be aware of your self – how your body feels, what's going through your mind, etc. Don't do anything, just breathe and watch.

Step 3: Slowly expand your awareness to fill the whole room. Imagine it as some kind of light or energy that is spreading out from you, filling the room, surrounding all the other people and things in the room.

Step 4: When you feel like it, begin making sounds. Play a short improvisation together.

FIFTEEN

Solo Exercises

Although this workbook is primarily about improvising with others, it is just as useful to make improvisation a part of your solo practicing routine. In addition to the exercises in this chapter, many of the group improvisation ideas in this book can also be used in your solo improvisation.

Making Sounds

Any and all sounds are useful information, and as you listen to them, they become a part of your personal universe of sound. This includes the sounds around you all the time, as well as all styles of music. When you hear something that you like or seems interesting to you, listen to it a lot. Sing along with it. Learn how to play it or imitate it on your instrument.

Exercise 120: Alien Instrument

Step 1: Take a moment to imagine you are a person from another culture or another planet. Forget for a moment all you know about your instrument.

Step 2: Now look at it. What an amazing and wonderful artifact!

Step 3: Play with your instrument and all the parts of your instrument from this perspective. When you find a sound that interests you, explore it. What are all the ways you can get sounds from this artifact? What are all the different sounds you can make? What do they remind you of? What do you feel when you hear that kind of sound?

Awareness

The seeds of creative, joyful improvisation with the world are within us at every moment. The improviser's goal is for the creative impulse and its expression to occur simultaneously, with no gap between what you want to do and doing it. Like moving your arm, the desire becomes the action.

One step toward this goal is awareness. Here are a few simple exercises in awareness, one related to listening to music, (though it can be as effectively practiced in any interaction you may have) and one about listening to yourself play music.

Exercise 121: Listening to Others

Step 1: Practice listening to others playing. Let your awareness be full of what you are listening to.

Step 2: Watch your response to it, not on an intellectual or verbal level, but on a gut level. Do not judge, just let your awareness focus on the music and your response to it.

Exercise 122: Listening to Yourself

Step 1: Play a note. Be aware of the sound you are creating.

*Tip: This exercise will help you develop the concentration and awareness needed to be able to **be** your note. When you can do this, even a single note or simple phrase can be a profound expression of your self!*

Step 2: Hold this awareness in your mind. Become the note you are playing, as much as you can. Let there be nothing in your mind except your awareness of that note. Whenever you drift away from that awareness, bring yourself back to it, gently, without judging. Let your intuitive knowledge bring the sound you are hearing outside, closer and closer to the sound you desire.

Self Expression

Never waste your time in rote practicing of technique. If you practice as an improviser, every moment of playing your instrument can be a creative expression. You can use the discipline of practicing to create a body of experience that enriches your expression in the moment, or you can use the same practice discipline to create a bag of pre-programmed habits. The difference is not what scales, licks, changes, or sounds you practice, but where you stand in relation to them while practicing.

Exercise 123: Long Tones

Step 1: Pick a note.

Step 2: Play it as many ways as you can, experimenting with things like:
  ‣ Length of the note (long, short, and everything in between)
  ‣ Dynamics (loud, soft, <, >, <>, ><, etc.)
  ‣ Articulation (how many ways can you begin and end the note?)
  ‣ Timbre (what kind of sounds can you make?)
  ‣ Vibrato (what kind of movement happens within the note?)

▸ Vocal Inflections (how many ways can you play with the sound, slide up and down, make it scream, cry, laugh, etc.?)

Step 3: Have fun playing with all these different ways to create a single sound. Combine them. Make up your own. This exercise will give you instantaneous access to a huge personal library of sounds and colors.

Step 4: As you play the sounds, be aware of how your body, mind, feelings, and memories react. When you vary the parameters of the sound, how do you react to the change? Practicing this awareness will give you an intuitive knowledge of the meaning that various sounds have for you.

Exercise 124: Patterns

When you are first practicing a technical exercise like a scale, arpeggio, or other pattern, practice it slowly. Pay attention to how it feels when you play each note and when you stop at each note. Once you have the pattern under your fingers, and the sound in your ears, make every time that you practice it an exploration and an improvisation.

Step 1: Make melodies using the pattern.

Step 2: Play it in different rhythms, grooves, and tempos.

Step 3: Explore it while varying dynamics, articulation, etc., as suggested in Exercise 123: Long Tones.

INDEX OF EXERCISES

1. One Sound, pg. 17

2. One Sound at a Time, pg. 18

3. One Sound, Anywhere in the Beat, pg. 18

4. Any Sound, Anywhere in the Beat, pg. 19

5. One Sound, Change Tempo, pg. 19

6. One Sound, Different Feels, pg. 19

7. One Sound, Together, pg. 19

8. More Than One Sound, Together, pg. 20

9. Ostinato Groove, pg. 21

10. Mutating Groove, pg. 21

11. Dueling Grooves, pg. 22

12. Mirroring, pg. 23

13. Ending, pg. 24

14. Awareness 1, pg. 25

15. Hearing Relationship, pg. 29

16. How Many Relationships Can You Find?, pg. 30

AFTERWORD

I love to improvise. I love being completely immersed in the flow of an improvisation. I love those transcendent moments of feeling joyfully and vibrantly alive, when inspiration and creation seem effortlessly connected. My passion for understanding and extending those moments has led me to music, to free improvisation, and to this wonderful opportunity to share some of what I've learned with you.

I believe free improvisation is a natural, practical part of life, best understood using language we all know and intuitively understand. It's not just for jazz musicians, or even just for students, teachers, and musicians of all genres. An intimate understanding of improvisation is good for everyone, because the better improvisers we are, the better we are at creating our lives.

Each moment of improvisation tells me a simple truth, a truth children instinctively know and live by, that is too often buried beneath the complexities of daily life. Mister Rogers speaks to this truth in the simplest and most profound way, when he says: "It just feels good to be alive when you're playing and making up things."

May your improvisational journeys give you many more moments when it just feels good to be alive!

Tom Hall, 2009